The Grateful Hearts Method

The Grateful Hearts Method

A Faith-Rooted System for Growing Real Food with Integrity, Protection, and Abundance

By Joann Comer-Conwell

Copyright © 2026 Joann Comer-Conwell

All rights reserved.
No part of this book may be reproduced, stored in a retrieval system, or transmitted in any form or by any means—electronic, mechanical, photocopying, recording, or otherwise—without prior written permission of the author, except for brief quotations in reviews.

This book is sold subject to the condition that it shall not, by way of trade or otherwise, be lent, resold, hired out, or otherwise circulated without the publisher's prior consent in any form of binding or cover other than that in which it is published.

The information contained in this book is for educational purposes only. The author is not a medical professional, agricultural extension agent, or legal advisor. Readers are encouraged to use their own judgment and consult appropriate professionals when necessary. The author assumes no responsibility for errors, omissions, or outcomes resulting from the use of this information.

Scripture quotations are taken from the Holy Bible.
All scripture references are used for inspirational and educational purposes.

ISBN: 979-8-9993039-2-9
Printed in the United States of America

Dedication & Acknowledgments

Above all, I give thanks to God, whose design for provision was never meant to be complicated, fear-driven, or detached from relationship. This work exists because of His faithfulness, and it is offered with a grateful heart.

Most especially, this book is dedicated to my husband, Mike. He is the strength God gave me to do this work. Without his support, encouragement, and willingness to stand beside me through every garden, every season, and every challenge, not a single garden would have been built. His steadiness, protection, and love made this work possible, and I am deeply grateful for him.

This book is dedicated to every person who has ever looked at their plate and wondered where their food truly came from—and then felt called to do something about it. It is also dedicated to those who grow quietly, give generously, and work faithfully, often without recognition, including the helpers who lend their hands and the landowners who extend trust.

This work is carried out through Grateful Hearts Givings NJ Nonprofit, whose mission is rooted in feeding people with dignity, integrity, and compassion. Every garden, every lesson, and every harvest described in these pages reflects the purpose of this nonprofit—to grow food, build community, and serve others with grateful hearts.

I acknowledge the wisdom passed down through generations of gardeners who understood that food is not just nourishment for the body, but a responsibility of the heart.

Introduction

When Gratitude Becomes a Way of Growing

Most gardening books begin with soil.

They tell you what to plant, when to plant it, and how to coax the greatest yield from the ground. They assume you already have land, time, energy, and a sense of certainty about why you're growing food in the first place.

This book is different.

The Grateful Hearts Method™ does not begin with seeds or soil. It begins with a question many people are quietly asking:

Why doesn't food feel safe anymore?

You may not have the language for it, but you feel it every time you read a label you don't fully trust, every time produce looks perfect but tastes empty, and every time you wonder what long-term effects those choices may carry. You may feel drawn to growing your own food, not out of trend or nostalgia, but out of a desire for clarity, honesty, and peace.

If that sounds familiar, you are not alone.

This book was written for people who want real food but also want to live real lives. People who may not own land, may not have unlimited money, may not have perfect health, and may not want to be driven by fear or extremes. It was written for those who believe that how we grow food matters just as much as what we grow.

At its heart, The Grateful Hearts Method™ is a system of integrity.

It teaches you how to grow food in a way that honors God, respects people, protects your labor, and carries provision forward without panic or pressure. It addresses the parts of gardening that are rarely discussed—permission, boundaries, fairness, burnout, and sustainability of the gardener—not because they are uncomfortable, but because they are essential.

This is not a book about doing more.

It is a book about doing things right.

You will learn how to begin where you are, grow only what you can manage, build help without being taken advantage of, and design a garden that still works when life inevitably shifts. You will be encouraged to grow with gratitude rather than urgency, wisdom rather than perfection, and faith rather than fear.

The chapters that follow are intentionally ordered. Each one builds on the last, starting not with dirt, but with understanding. Because before you plant anything in the ground, you must first plant clarity in your thinking.

When gratitude becomes the foundation, growth becomes sustainable.

Welcome to

The Grateful Hearts Method™

The Grateful Hearts Method™

The Grateful Hearts Method™ is a faith-rooted, integrity-based system for growing real food, building trusted help, protecting land and labor, and carrying provision forward from one season to the next — even when starting with limited space, money, or strength.

This method is built on the belief that how food is grown matters as much as what is grown. It prioritizes gratitude before growth, integrity before expansion, people before plants, protection before production, and continuity before excess.

The Grateful Hearts Method™ exists to help ordinary people grow food in extraordinary ways — with wisdom, fairness, and faith guiding every decision.

The Grateful Hearts Method™: An Overview

The Grateful Hearts Method™ is not a gardening shortcut or a production formula. It is a complete, values-driven approach to growing food that begins long before the first seed is planted and continues long after the harvest is complete.

At its core, the method teaches that most gardens fail not because of poor soil, but because of poor structure, unclear boundaries, broken trust, and unsustainable expectations placed on the gardener.

This method emphasizes five guiding pillars:

Gratitude — Beginning with appreciation for what you already have, rather than pressure to produce more.

Integrity — Growing and sharing food in ways that are honest, fair, and respectful of people and property.

Protection — Safeguarding land access, labor, harvest, and relationships before problems arise.

Stewardship — Designing gardens that serve the gardener's life, health, and capacity over time.

Continuity — Carrying food, seeds, and knowledge forward from one season to the next without fear.

The Grateful Hearts Method™ teaches how to grow real food the way God intended it to be grown — without chemicals, without panic, and without compromising values. It shows how to find space when you do not own land, how to build help without being taken advantage of, how to honor those who labor alongside you, and how to create abundance that lasts.

Each book in this series explores a different aspect of the method, but all are rooted in the same foundation: food grown with grateful hearts nourishes more than the body.

What This Book Is - and What It Is Not

This book is a practical guide rooted in faith, integrity, and lived experience. It is written for people who want to grow real food without fear, extremes, or exploitation.

This book is:

- A values-driven system for growing food with clarity and purpose
- A guide for people with limited space, limited resources, or limited strength
- Grounded in faith without being preachy
- Honest about the realities of land access, help, boundaries, and burnout
- Focused on sustainability of both the garden and the gardener

This book is not:

- A chemical-based growing manual
- A get-rich-quick gardening or farming guide
- A perfection-driven or productivity-obsessed approach
- A book that assumes you own land, have unlimited time, or perfect health
- A substitute for wisdom, patience, or personal responsibility

This book does not promise maximum yields.
It promises thoughtful growth.

It does not teach shortcuts.
It teaches structure.

And it does not separate faith from real life — because real life is exactly where faith belongs.

Chapter One

Why Food No Longer Feels Safe

When certainty disappeared from the table

There was a time when food did not require courage.

You didn't need to research it.
You didn't need to question it.
You didn't need to read labels with a furrowed brow or search for hidden meanings behind reassuring words.

Food came from the ground, from familiar hands, from soil that had been worked season after season. You knew who grew it, where it came from, and how it was handled. Even when times were hard, food still felt honest.

Today, that certainty is gone.

Many people cannot quite explain when it happened, only that it did. Somewhere between convenience and mass production, food stopped feeling trustworthy. We now stand in grocery store aisles surrounded by abundance, yet unsure of what we are actually taking home. Fruits and vegetables look flawless, uniform, almost too perfect—yet often lack flavor, nourishment, and reassurance.

If you have ever picked up a tomato that looked beautiful but tasted like water, you already understand this loss.

Food no longer feels safe—not because we lack it, but because we no longer know it.

And when food feels uncertain, something deeper begins to shift. The table, once a place of comfort, becomes a place of quiet doubt. What am I feeding my body? What am I feeding my family? What is really in this food, and what will it do over time?

These questions are not fear-based. They are instinctive. They come from a place of care.

This chapter is not about blaming systems or shaming choices. It is about acknowledging a truth many people feel but rarely name food insecurity today is often emotional and spiritual before it is physical.

Grateful Hearts Principle

When food loses transparency, people lose peace. Restoring trust in what we eat begins by restoring our relationship with the source.

This method begins here because gardening is not just about producing food. It is about rebuilding trust—trust in the soil, trust in the process, and trust in our own ability to participate wisely.

What You Need to Know

Modern food systems are designed for efficiency, scale, and profit. These goals are not inherently wrong, but they are rarely aligned with transparency, nourishment, or long-term health. When food is grown far from the people who eat it, treated through processes we cannot see, and transported through systems we do not control, trust naturally erodes.

Labels attempt to fill this gap. Organic. Natural. Non-GMO. These words are meant to reassure, yet they often raise more questions than they answer. What does "natural" truly mean? Who defines it? What practices are allowed, and which are not?

For many people, the result is quiet resignation. They buy the best they can afford. They hope for the best. They tell themselves this is simply how things are now.

But something inside still resists.

That resistance is not rebellion—it is remembrance. It is the memory, whether personal or inherited, that food was once more than a product. It was a relationship between people, land, and provision.

When you feel drawn to grow your own food, you are not chasing a trend. You are responding to a loss of connection. You are seeking clarity where there has been confusion, simplicity where there has been complication, and honesty where there has been opacity.

This is why The Grateful Hearts Method™ does not begin with soil or seeds. If you do not first understand why food feels unsafe, you may rush into gardening for the wrong reasons—out of fear, urgency, or pressure rather than wisdom.

Gardens built on fear often burn out their caretakers.
Gardens built on gratitude endure.

Hard Truth

Growing your own food will not automatically bring peace if it is rooted in fear.

Peace comes when you grow with clarity, purpose, and protection. This book will never tell you to grow everything at once, replace all store-bought food overnight, or carry the weight of perfection. That mindset leads to exhaustion, not freedom.

How This Looks in Real Life

Consider two people who decide to start a garden.

The first is overwhelmed. They are frightened by what they read online, convinced that everything in the store is harmful, and determined to grow as much food as possible as quickly as possible. They buy seeds they do not eat, plant more than they can manage, and push themselves beyond their limits. When pests arrive or weather shifts, discouragement sets in. The garden becomes another source of stress.

The second person pauses. They ask better questions. They choose to grow a small amount of food they already enjoy. They observe how it grows, how it tastes, and how it makes them feel. They keep notes. They allow themselves to learn. Over time, confidence replaces anxiety.

The difference is not intelligence or access.
The difference is posture.

The Grateful Hearts Method™ teaches you to grow from a place of steadiness. You are not trying to outrun the world. You are learning to anchor yourself within it.

Food safety is not restored by control alone. It is restored by relationship—relationship with the soil, the plant, the season, and your own capacity.

Scripture in Practice

"Better a little with the fear of the Lord than great wealth with turmoil." — Proverbs 15:16

Peace does not come from excess, but from provision received with wisdom and reverence.

Garden Wisdom

When food begins to feel unsafe, the answer is not panic—it is participation.

Participation restores agency.
Agency restores peace.

Bringing It Together

This chapter is not meant to convince you that everything is broken. It is meant to validate what you already sense: that something meaningful has been lost in how we relate to food, and that the desire to grow is a healthy response—not an extreme one.

Before you ever choose a garden spot, before you look for land, before you buy seeds or soil, understand this: you are not trying to escape the world—you are learning how to live more wisely within it.

Food no longer feels safe because it no longer feels personal. Gardening restores that personal connection one decision at a time.

In the next chapter, we will talk about gratitude—not as a feeling, but as a foundation. Because how you begin determines how well your garden will hold when life inevitably presses against it.

Pause & Reflect

What was the first moment you remember questioning the food you eat, and what did that moment awaken in you?

Bringing It Together

Chapter Two

Gratitude Is the Beginning of Abundance

Why how you begin determines
how well you grow

Gratitude is often treated as a feeling—something you have after things go well.

In gardening, gratitude must come first.

Not after the harvest.
Not after success.
Not after everything turns out the way you hoped.

Gratitude is the posture you bring to work before the first seed is planted. It shapes how you plan, how you respond to challenges, and how you measure success. Without it, even a thriving garden can leave you exhausted, resentful, or restless. With it, even a small harvest can feel sufficient.

Many people begin gardening from a place of urgency. They feel pressure to fix everything at once—to grow more, do more, replace more, and prove more. That urgency often disguises itself as motivation, but it carries a hidden cost. Gardens built on urgency demand constant effort. Gardens built on gratitude allow room for growth.

This chapter is about establishing that foundation.

Before you choose land, before you decide what to grow, before you involve other people, you must understand this
truth: abundance is not created by how much you produce, but by how you relate to what you have.

Grateful Hearts Principle

Gratitude creates abundance by aligning effort with peace.

When gratitude leads, growth becomes steady instead of frantic. You stop measuring success by volume alone and begin measuring it by sustainability, integrity, and continuity.

What You Need to Know

In modern culture, abundance is often defined by excess. More food. More yield. More efficiency. More output. Gardening advice frequently reflects this mindset, encouraging maximum production in the smallest possible space, faster harvests, and constant expansion.

The problem is not ambition. The problem is misalignment.

When abundance is defined only by quantity, gardeners are pushed beyond their limits. They grow food they do not eat, manage more space than they can maintain, and depend on constant outside inputs to keep everything going. Over time, what began as empowerment turns into obligation.

Gratitude shifts that equation.

When you begin with gratitude, you grow with awareness. You pay attention to what you already have—your space, your energy, your time, your health, and your help. You choose growth that fits your life instead of forcing your life to fit the garden.

This is why The Grateful Hearts Method™ teaches you to begin with appreciation rather than aspiration. Appreciation grounds you. Aspiration without grounding leads to burnout.

Gratitude also changes how you view limitations. Instead of seeing them as obstacles, you begin to see them as guides. Limited space encourages intentional planting. Limited energy encourages smarter design. Limited time encourages focus. These constraints do not diminish abundance—they define it.

Abundance, in this method, is not about producing everything. It is about producing what is right, at the right time, in the right measure.

Hard Truth

Gardens that start from pressure eventually turn into burdens.

When you feel rushed to prove something through your garden—whether to yourself or others—you are more likely to overcommit, ignore warning signs, and resent the very work you once felt called to do.

How This Looks in Real Life

Imagine two gardeners beginning at the same time.

The first begins with a list of everything they want to grow. Tomatoes, peppers, herbs, greens, root crops—more than they realistically eat. They fill every available space and commit themselves to maintaining it all. At first, the garden looks impressive. Over time, missed watering, pest issues, and fatigue begin to take their toll. The gardener feels behind, even when the garden is producing.

The second gardener begins with gratitude. They take inventory. They note how much space they actually have, how much food they realistically consume, and how much time they can reasonably give. They choose a small number of crops they enjoy and plant only those. They observe, adjust, and expand slowly. Their garden grows alongside their confidence.

The difference is not skill.
The difference is beginning from contentment instead of comparison.

Gratitude allows you to grow within your capacity. Capacity can increase over time, but it cannot be forced.

Scripture in Practice

"Give, and it will be given to you. A good measure, pressed down, shaken together and running over, will be poured into your lap." — Luke 6:38

Abundance flows when we steward what we have with open hands rather than clenched ones.

Garden Wisdom

Gratitude prevents you from turning growth into a test you must pass.

When you are grateful for what you can manage today, you create space to grow tomorrow without regret.

Bringing It Together

Gratitude is not passive. It is a deliberate choice to grow with awareness rather than ambition alone. It asks different questions: What can I care for well? What fits my life right now? What allows me to continue year after year?

When you begin with gratitude, your garden becomes a partner instead of a taskmaster. It works with you, not against you. This foundation prepares you for the practical decisions that follow—what to grow, where to grow it, and how to involve others without strain.

In the next chapter, we will talk about a guiding mindset that protects both the gardener and the garden over time: doing the best you can, until you can do better. This principle frees you from perfection while keeping you rooted in progress.

Pause & Reflect

What expectations are you carrying into your garden that may need to be replaced with gratitude?

Chapter Three

Do the Best You Can

Until You Can Do Better

Why progress matters more than perfection

Perfection stops more gardens than poor soil ever could.

Many people delay starting because they believe they are not ready. They wait for the right tools, the right space, the right knowledge, the right season, or the right circumstances. They tell themselves they will begin once everything is lined up and ideal.

That moment rarely comes.

Life does not pause to make room for perfect beginnings. Health fluctuates. Finances shift. Time stretches thin. And yet the desire to grow—to participate, to provide, to reconnect—remains.

This chapter exists to remove that barrier.

Doing the best you can until you can do better is not an excuse for carelessness. It is a commitment to forward movement without shame. It is the understanding that growth happens through participation, not preparation alone.

The Grateful Hearts Method™ is built for real people living real lives. It does not require you to start at the finish line. It requires you to start where you are.

Grateful Hearts Principle

Faithful progress matters more than flawless execution.

When you do the best, you can with what you have today, you create the conditions to do better tomorrow.

What You Need to Know

Many gardening resources unintentionally create pressure. They present ideal conditions as prerequisites rather than goals. Perfect soil mixes, specialized equipment, and comprehensive knowledge are often portrayed as necessary starting points instead of outcomes developed over time.

This approach discourages beginners and exhausts seasoned growers.

The truth is simpler and kinder: most successful gardeners began imperfectly. They learned through observation, mistakes, and adjustment. They built skill gradually, not instantly.

Doing the best you can until you can do better means making informed choices within your current capacity. It means acknowledging limits without allowing them to become excuses. It also means resisting comparison—especially to gardens that are further along, better funded, or more visible.

Comparison distorts progress. Gratitude restores it.

This principle protects you from paralysis. It gives you permission to start small, refine as you go, and grow into the work rather than rushing ahead of it. Over time, experience replaces anxiety, and clarity replaces overwhelm.

Growth that lasts is almost always quiet at the beginning.

Hard Truth

Waiting to begin until everything is perfect is a decision to never begin at all.

Progress requires participation, not readiness.

How This Looks in Real Life

Consider a gardener who wants to grow food but feels overwhelmed by information. They read conflicting advice about soil amendments, pest control, and planting schedules. Instead of choosing one manageable step, they do nothing, afraid of doing it wrong.

Now consider another gardener facing the same uncertainty. They choose one container, one plant they enjoy eating, and one simple approach. They observe how it grows. They note what works and what does not. Over time, they adjust. They improve. They expand carefully.

The difference is not access to information.
The difference is willingness to act without guarantees.

Doing the best you can mean using the soil you already have instead of the soil you wish you had. It may mean growing fewer plants than recommended. It may mean asking for help sooner than you planned. None of these choices represent failure. They represent wisdom

This principle also applies when circumstances change. Illness, fatigue, or unexpected responsibilities may require you to scale back. Doing less for a season does not undo progress. It preserves it.

Gardens that last are built with flexibility, not force.

Scripture in Practice

"The plans of the diligent lead surely to abundance, but everyone who is hasty comes only to poverty." -Proverbs 21:5

Steady, thoughtful effort produces lasting provision.

Garden Wisdom

Improvement is only possible once you begin.

Waiting to do it perfectly keeps you from doing it at all.

Bringing It Together

Doing the best you can until you can do better is a posture of humility and trust. It acknowledges that growth is a process, not a performance. It frees you from the fear of mistakes and invites you into learning.

This mindset protects both the garden and the gardener. It allows room for seasons of expansion and seasons of rest. It honors the reality that capacity changes, but commitment remains.

In the next chapter, we will move from mindset to decision-making by addressing a principle that prevents overwhelm and waste from the very beginning: growing only what you eat.

Pause & Reflect

Where are you holding yourself back because you believe you need to do more before you are allowed to begin?

Chapter Four

Only Grow What You Eat

Why simplicity protects both the garden and the gardener

One of the quickest ways to overwhelm a garden is to grow food you do not actually eat.

This often happens with the best intentions. A seed catalog arrives filled with beautiful photos and promises of abundance. Advice from others adds enthusiasm—you should try this, this grows easily, everyone plants that. Before long, a garden is filled with crops chosen out of curiosity, pressure, or optimism rather than purpose.

What follows is predictable.

Plants grow that no one enjoys eating. Harvests go unused. Time is spent caring for crops that do not serve the household or the mission. The garden begins to feel like work instead of provision.

The Grateful Hearts Method™ prevents this problem from the very beginning with one simple, protective principle: only grow what you eat.

This chapter is not about limiting yourself. It is about honoring your time, your energy, and the reason you are growing food in the first place.

Grateful Hearts Principle

Purposeful growing creates sustainable abundance.

When every plant in your garden has a clear place at your table, the garden remains manageable, meaningful, and nourishing.

What You Need to Know

Gardens often fail not because they are too small, but because they are too scattered. Growing a wide variety of crops without intention divides attention, increases maintenance, and complicates harvest and storage. Over time, this leads to frustration and waste.

Growing only what you eat brings focus.

When you choose crops based on actual use rather than interest, your garden becomes aligned with your daily life. Watering, harvesting, and preserving all serve a clear purpose. The work feels justified because the results are enjoyed.

This principle is especially important when space, money, or physical strength is limited. Every container, bed, or crate must earn its place. Growing food that will not be eaten quietly steals resources from food that will.

This does not mean you can never try something new. It means experimentation comes after stability. Once you have established a core group of crops you reliably grow and consume, you can expand thoughtfully. Until then, restraint is wisdom.

The Grateful Hearts Method™ encourages growers to build a solid foundation over one to two seasons before branching out. This timeline allows habits to form, confidence to grow, and systems to stabilize.

Abundance built slowly lasts longer.

Hard Truth

A garden full of plants you do not eat is not abundance—it is obligation.

When food goes unused, discouragement follows.

How This Looks in Real Life

Imagine a gardener with limited space who decides to grow tomatoes, peppers, herbs, greens, squash, root crops, and several novelty vegetables they have never cooked before. At harvest time, the familiar crops are used, while the unfamiliar ones linger, spoil, or are given away reluctantly.

Contrast this with a gardener who begins by listing the foods they eat every week. They choose three or four staple crops and focus on growing them well. Harvests are anticipated, meals are planned around them, and nothing feels wasted.

The second gardener may grow fewer varieties, but their garden feeds them more consistently.

This approach also benefits those growing food for others. When gardens are part of a nonprofit mission like Grateful Hearts Givings NJ Nonprofit, intentional growing ensures that donated food is familiar, useful, and welcomed. Dignity is preserved when recipients receive foods they know how to prepare and enjoy.

Growing only what is eaten respects both the giver and the receiver.

Scripture in Practice

"Gather of it, each one of you, as much as he can eat." — Exodus 16:16

Provision was never meant to be excessive or wasteful, but sufficient and purposeful.

Garden Wisdom

The most productive garden is not the one with the most varieties, but the one where nothing goes to waste.

Bringing It Together

Only growing what you eat simplifies every part of the gardening process. Planning becomes clearer. Maintenance becomes lighter. Harvest becomes joyful rather than stressful. Preservation becomes manageable instead of overwhelming.

This principle protects you from burnout and keeps your garden aligned with its purpose. It ensures that the effort you invest returns nourishment, not regret.

As your confidence and capacity grow, so can your garden. But expansion should always be intentional, guided by experience rather than impulse.

In the next chapter, we will explore a tool that helps you remember what works, refine what doesn't, and grow wiser with each season: keeping a garden journal.

Pause & Reflect

What foods do you eat most often, and how might your garden better reflect those habits?

Chapter Five

Why Every Gardener Needs a Journal

How memory becomes wisdom

Gardens teach constantly—but only if you remember what they show you.

Many lessons arrive quietly: a plant that thrives in one spot and struggles in another, a harvest that comes earlier than expected, a pest problem that appears at the same time each year. These patterns are easy to notice in the moment and just as easy to forget once the season passes.

That forgetting is costly.

Without a record, gardeners repeat mistakes they already paid to learn. They re-experiment with the same problems, relearn the same timing, and second-guess choices they already tested. Over time, frustration replaces confidence, and progress feels slower than it needs to be.

A garden journal changes that.

In The Grateful Hearts Method™, journaling is not an optional hobby add-on. It is a tool of stewardship. It transforms experience into guidance and effort into accumulated wisdom.

Grateful Hearts Principle

What you record, you retain.
What you retain, you refine.

A journal turns seasons into teachers rather than tests.

What You Need to Know

Gardening is seasonal by nature, which makes memory unreliable. What feels obvious in July can be hazy by February. Without notes, gardeners often rely on guesswork instead of evidence.

A journal provides continuity.

It does not need to be elaborate or artistic. It needs to be honest and consistent. Dates, observations, outcomes, and reflections are enough. Over time, patterns emerge that no book or website can provide, because they are specific to your space, your climate, and your capacity.

This is especially important when gardens are shared, borrowed, or part of a larger mission. When multiple people are involved, written records prevent confusion and miscommunication. Decisions become traceable. Improvements become intentional.

A journal also protects you from comparison. Instead of measuring your garden against someone else's, you measure it against its own progress. That shift builds confidence and patience.

The Grateful Hearts Method™ encourages journaling because it honors learning as a process. You are not expected to know everything. You are expected to notice and remember.

Hard Truth

If you do not write it down, you are likely to relearn the same lesson again.

Time spent journaling saves time spent fixing avoidable mistakes.

How This Looks in Real Life

Consider a gardener who struggles with pests every summer. Each year, the issue feels new and urgent. Solutions are tried at random, often too late. The frustration repeats.

Now consider a gardener who notes when pests appear, which plants are affected, and what responses work. Over time, prevention replaces reaction. Confidence replaces panic.

The same applies to harvest timing, watering routines, soil improvements, and even personal capacity. A journal shows not only what the garden needs, but what the gardener can realistically manage.

For nonprofit work through Grateful Hearts Givings NJ Nonprofit, journaling becomes even more valuable. It preserves institutional memory. It allows future gardens, volunteers, and seasons to benefit from lessons already learned. Wisdom is shared, not lost.

A journal ensures that progress continues even when people change.

Scripture in Practice

"Write the vision; make it plain." — Habakkuk 2:2

Clarity grows when intentions and outcomes are recorded.

Garden Wisdom

Your garden will tell you what it needs.
A journal helps you remember to listen.

Bringing It Together

A garden journal is not about perfection or performance. It is about attention. It creates a conversation between seasons, allowing each year to build on the last rather than starting over.

This practice reinforces patience and progress. It turns experience into insight and mistakes into guidance. Over time, the journal becomes one of the most valuable tools you own—not because it contains answers, but because it preserves learning.

In the next chapter, we will take that recorded knowledge and apply it to a practical decision that affects every garden: choosing where to grow when you do not own land.

Pause & Reflect

What information from past seasons do you wish you had written down—and how might a journal change your next growing year?

Chapter Six

You Don't Need to Own Land to Grow Food

Rethinking access, space, and possibility

One of the most common reasons people believe they cannot grow food is simple: they do not own land.

This belief quietly shuts the door before the conversation even begins. It convinces people that growing food is reserved for homeowners, people with acreage, or those with ideal conditions. As a result, the desire to grow is often dismissed as unrealistic before it is ever explored.

But land ownership has never been the true requirement for growing food.

Throughout history, food has been grown wherever people had access, permission, and care—small yards, shared spaces, community plots, borrowed corners, and overlooked ground. What mattered was not ownership, but stewardship.

The Grateful Hearts Method™ begins by separating ownership from access. When you understand that distinction, possibility opens.

Grateful Hearts Principle

Access creates opportunity when it is approached with humility and care.

You do not need to own land to grow food—you need space that can be respected and stewarded.

What You Need to Know

There are far more places to grow food than most people realize. Many gardens never exist simply because those spaces are never considered.

Small spaces are often the first overlooked option. Patios, porches, balconies, side yards, and narrow strips of land can support meaningful food production when used thoughtfully. These spaces may not look like traditional gardens, but they can still produce nourishment.

Borrowed spaces offer another opportunity. Neighbors, friends, faith communities, and local property owners often have unused land they are not prepared to maintain themselves. When approached with clarity and respect, these spaces can become productive ground.

Community spaces expand the possibilities even further. Shared gardens, nonprofit-supported plots, and communal growing areas allow people without private access to participate in food production together. These spaces often grow more than food—they grow connection.

The key is understanding that space is not defined by size or ownership. It is defined by use.

The Grateful Hearts Method™ teaches that before asking how to grow, you must first ask where growth is possible. That question alone reshapes what you see around you.

Hard Truth

Waiting for ideal land often means waiting forever.

Food grows where people are willing to look differently at space.

How This Looks in Real Life

A person living in a small apartment assumes gardening is not possible. They overlook a sunny stoop that could support containers. Another person passes unused ground every day behind a building without ever considering that it might be offered for use.

Someone else believes community gardens are "for other people," not realizing they exist precisely for those without land of their own.

When perspective shifts, options multiply.

For work done through Grateful Hearts Givings NJ Nonprofit, this mindset is essential. Many of the gardens that serve others are grown on land that was once unused or ignored. The ability to recognize potential space is often the first step in serving well.

Access begins with awareness.

Scripture in Practice

"The earth is the Lord's, and everything in it." — Psalm 24:1

Stewardship begins when we remember that land is entrusted, not possessed.

Garden Wisdom

Most gardens don't fail because space is unavailable.
They fail because possibility is never explored.

Bringing It Together

You do not need to own land to grow food. You need openness—to see space differently, to consider shared ground, and to recognize opportunity where others see none.

This chapter is about expanding what you believe is possible. Once space is identified, the next step is learning how to honor it.

In the next chapter, we will focus on what it means to garden on someone else's property with integrity—why cleanliness, care, and presentation matter, and how respect becomes the currency that keeps doors open.

Pause & Reflect

What spaces around you—small, borrowed, or shared—might support food growth if you looked at them with fresh eyes?

Chapter Seven

Gardening on Someone Else's Property with Integrity

Why respect is seen before it is trusted

When you garden on land that does not belong to you, your garden speaks before you do.

Long before a conversation happens, before explanations are offered, and before trust is extended, the condition of the garden sends a message. Order communicates care. Cleanliness communicates responsibility. Beauty communicates respect.

Integrity, in borrowed spaces, must be visible.

Many people believe integrity is proven through words or intentions. In reality, it is proven through consistency and presentation. When you are working on someone else's property, how the garden looks is often the deciding factor in whether access continues or disappears.

The Grateful Hearts Method™ treats appearance not as vanity, but as stewardship. A well-kept garden protects relationships just as much as it protects plants.

Grateful Hearts Principle

Respect must be visible in shared spaces.

When a garden looks cared for, trust grows naturally.

What You Need to Know

Gardening on someone else's property carries a responsibility beyond food production. You are representing not only yourself, but the values behind the work. Messy, neglected, or chaotic gardens create doubt—even when intentions are good.

Appearance matters because it reassures property owners that their space is being honored.

Clean edges, orderly planting, managed weeds, and the removal of clutter all communicate the same message: this land is being respected. These details signal reliability far more clearly than promises ever could.

Integrity in borrowed gardens also shows up in consistency. A garden that starts neatly but becomes neglected over time erodes confidence. Regular maintenance, seasonal cleanup, and attention to presentation demonstrate commitment.

This is especially important when gardens are connected to nonprofit work through Grateful Hearts Givings NJ Nonprofit. Community trust is fragile. One poorly maintained space can undo goodwill built elsewhere. Integrity must be practiced everywhere, every time.

The goal is not perfection.
The goal is, care that is obvious.

Hard Truth

A messy garden on borrowed land costs trust quickly.

Once trust is damaged, access is rarely restored.

How This Looks in Real Life

A gardener is allowed to use a section of a neighbor's yard. At first, the space is tidy and organized. Over time, tools are left out, weeds spread, and harvested plants are left unattended. Though no rules were broken, discomfort grows. Eventually, permission is quietly withdrawn.

Now consider another situation.

A gardener maintains clean borders, removes debris promptly, and leaves the space looking better than they found it. Even when harvest is light or challenges arise, the care is visible. The property owner feels respected rather than burdened.

The difference is not productivity.
The difference is presentation.

For shared or community gardens, the same principle applies. Neat gardens invite participation. Disorganized spaces discourage involvement. People are more willing to help when the work appears purposeful and cared for.

Integrity builds confidence when it is seen.

Scripture in Practice

"Whatever you do, do it heartily, as unto the Lord." — Colossians 3:23

Care given openly reflects respect offered sincerely.

Garden Wisdom

A garden that looks honored will continue to be allowed.

Respect is renewed every time the space is tended.

Bringing It Together

Gardening on someone else's property is a privilege, not a right. That privilege is maintained through visible care, thoughtful presentation, and consistent respect.

Integrity is not something you claim—it is something others observe. When your garden reflects order and attention, it builds trust quietly and steadily.

In the next chapter, we will address how integrity must also be protected in writing—why clear permission matters, how simple agreements safeguard effort, and when walking away is the wisest choice.

Pause & Reflect

If someone judged your garden today by appearance alone, what would it say about your respect for the space?

Chapter Eight

Get It in Writing — Always

Why clarity protects effort, relationships, and harvest

Good intentions do not protect your work.

Many gardening arrangements begin with friendly conversations, verbal agreements, and mutual excitement. Everything feels understood. Everyone is agreeable. The garden is planted with optimism.

And then something changes.

A property owner moves.
A family member steps in.
A misunderstanding arises.
A boundary that was never stated suddenly matters.

When nothing is in writing, the gardener has no protection—no matter how much time, effort, or care has already been invested.

The Grateful Hearts Method™ treats written permission not as mistrust, but as wisdom. A simple written agreement protects relationships by preventing confusion before it starts.

This chapter exists to save you from heartbreak that is entirely avoidable.

Grateful Hearts Principle

Clarity preserves peace.

When expectations are written, relationships are protected.

What You Need to Know

Written permission does not need to be complicated to be effective. In fact, the simpler it is, the better it works.

A basic permission letter should include only a few elements:

- The name of the property owner
- The name of the gardener or group
- A clear statement granting permission to garden
- The general location or size of the space
- The date the permission is given

Nothing more is required.

This letter is not a lease. It is not a contract. It is an acknowledgment of permission that protects both parties by making the arrangement clear.

One important detail matters greatly: avoid timelines whenever possible.

When permission letters include start and end dates, gardeners unknowingly place themselves at risk. Timelines create pressure. They restrict flexibility. They allow access to be withdrawn at the exact moment a garden becomes productive.

The Grateful Hearts Method™ encourages open-ended permission whenever possible. If an arrangement must end, it can be ended respectfully—but productivity should not be timed against a calendar that works against the gardener.

Written clarity does not lock people in.
It keeps people honest.

Hard Truth

If permission is not written down, it can be taken back without warning.

Labor given without protection is labor at risk.

How This Looks in Real Life

A gardener plants on borrowed land after a friendly conversation. Months later, the property owner decides to use the space for something else. The gardener is told to remove everything immediately. There is no recourse. The harvest is lost.

Now consider another gardener.

Before planting, they provide a simple permission letter. When circumstances change, the conversation is different. The agreement is referenced. Time is allowed for harvest. Respect replaces urgency.

For gardens grown through Grateful Hearts Givings NJ Nonprofit, written permission is essential. It protects donated labor, community trust, and the dignity of those served. Without documentation, nonprofit work becomes vulnerable to disruption that harms more than just plants.

Sometimes, the wisest decision is not to proceed at all.

If a property owner resists written permission, insists on strict timelines, or refuses clarity, that hesitation is information. Walking away early prevents deeper loss later.

Not every opportunity is worth the risk.

Scripture in Practice

"The prudent see danger and take refuge, but the simple keep going and pay the penalty." — Proverbs 22:3

Wisdom protects what effort alone cannot.

Garden Wisdom

A simple piece of paper can protect an entire season.

If clarity is resisted, protection is already missing.

Bringing It Together

Getting permission in writing is not about distrust. It is about stewardship. It honors the landowner, the gardener, and the work itself by making expectations visible and shared.

Written clarity prevents conflict, protects harvest, and allows gardens to grow without fear of sudden loss. It also gives gardeners the confidence to invest fully, knowing their effort is respected.

In the next chapter, we will shift from land access to garden design—exploring how to grow in ways that protect your body, your dignity, and your ability to continue even when strength changes.

Pause & Reflect

What boundaries or expectations would be easier to honor if they were written instead of assumed?

Chapter Nine

Garden Like You're 80

Designing for dignity, access, and longevity

Most gardens are designed for the gardener you wish you would always be.

They assume strength that never fades, energy that never dips, and health that never changes. They are built low to the ground, spread wide, and demand bending, lifting, kneeling, and constant exertion. In the early years, this may seem manageable. Over time, it becomes exhausting.

The truth is simple: life happens.

Illness arrives unexpectedly. Injuries slow movement. Energy fluctuates. Aging is not optional. And yet, gardens built without these realities in mind quietly push people out of the very work that once nourished them.

The Grateful Hearts Method™ approaches design differently.

Instead of asking what the strongest gardener can manage, it asks what the gardener can sustain. When you design as if you are already eighty years old, you create a garden that serves you for a lifetime—not just a season.

Grateful Hearts Principle

A garden should serve the gardener, not consume them.

Designing for dignity ensures longevity.

What You Need to Know

Design is not decoration. It is protection.

When a garden is physically demanding, it becomes fragile. It depends entirely on the gardener's strength staying the same year after year. That expectation is unrealistic and unfair. Eventually, something gives—and it is often the garden that is abandoned.

Designing with future needs in mind does not mean you expect decline. It means you respect reality.

Gardens that are easier to tend are more likely to be maintained consistently. Consistency matters more than intensity. Raised growing systems, accessible heights, and nearby seating allow work to continue even on low-energy days.

This principle is especially important for those growing food as part of service or nonprofit work through Grateful Hearts Givings NJ Nonprofit. Gardens meant to feed others must be reliable. Reliability requires designs that do not depend on peak physical condition.

Designing for dignity protects not just the gardener's body, but their commitment.

Hard Truth

Gardens that require constant bending, lifting, and strain eventually exclude the gardener.

If the garden cannot be tended during hard seasons, it is not sustainable.

How This Looks in Real Life

Consider two gardeners.

The first builds directly in the ground, spreading plants across a wide area. The work requires kneeling, bending, and long periods of standing. When health changes, the garden becomes unmanageable. Slowly, sections are neglected. Eventually, the entire space is abandoned.

The second gardener designs intentionally. Growing areas are raised to comfortable heights. Paths are clear and stable. A bench sits nearby for rest. Tools are stored within reach. On strong days, more work gets done. On weekdays, the garden remains accessible.

The difference is not motivation.
The difference is design.

Gardening like you're eighty does not limit productivity. It preserves it.

Scripture in Practice

"The wise woman builds her house." — Proverbs 14:1

Wisdom builds with the future in mind.

Garden Wisdom

If your garden only works on your strongest days, it will fail you on your weakest ones.

Design for continuity, not pride.

Bringing It Together

Gardening is meant to be life-giving, not draining. When design honors the gardener's body and capacity, the work remains accessible across seasons of strength and weakness.

Designing like you are eighty is an act of wisdom, not resignation. It creates space for rest, healing, and continued participation—no matter what life brings.

In the next chapter, we will look closely at one of the most practical ways to reduce strain and protect both body and harvest: avoiding the ground when you can.

Pause & Reflect

What parts of your current garden design might become difficult if your strength or health changed—and how could you adjust now to protect the future?

Chapter Ten

Avoiding the Ground When You Can

How elevation protects energy, plants, and persistence

Ground-level gardening is often treated as the default.

It is familiar. It is traditional. And for many gardeners, it is simply how things have always been done. But tradition does not always equal wisdom—especially when it comes to sustainability of both body and garden.

The Grateful Hearts Method™ encourages gardeners to question what is assumed. One of the most important questions is this: Does this garden need to be in the ground at all?

When growing is elevated—whether through containers, planters, or raised systems—the entire experience changes. Work becomes lighter. Access improves. Many pests are reduced. And the gardener gains control that ground-level gardens rarely offer.

Avoiding the ground when you can is not about convenience. It is about protection.

Grateful Hearts Principle

Elevation reduces strain and increases stewardship.

When the garden is lifted, both plants and people are protected.

What You Need to Know

Ground-level gardens demand physical labor that many gardeners underestimate. Bending, kneeling, and lifting are required constantly. Over time, these movements accumulate strain that can shorten a gardener's ability to continue.

Elevated growing systems shift that burden.

Containers, planters, milk crate gardens, and raised structures bring the garden closer to the gardener. This reduces physical stress while increasing visibility and control. Tasks become easier to manage in short periods rather than requiring long, exhausting sessions.

Elevation also changes how pests interact with the garden.

Many common pests—slugs, ground insects, and burrowing animals—have easier access to plants grown directly in the soil. Raised systems introduce barriers that discourage damage and make protection simpler.

Energy conservation is another overlooked benefit.

When gardens are compact and elevated, less movement is required. Watering takes less time. Harvesting is quicker. Maintenance becomes more efficient. These savings matter most during seasons when energy is limited.

The Grateful Hearts Method™ teaches that conserving the gardener's strength is an act of wisdom. Food production should not demand unnecessary exhaustion.

Hard Truth

Gardens that require excessive physical effort will eventually be abandoned.

Elevation extends the life of both the garden and the gardener.

How This Looks in Real Life

A gardener grows directly in the ground across a large space. Each visit requires bending, kneeling, and walking long distances. As fatigue increases, tasks are postponed. Weeds spread. Harvests are delayed.

Another gardener grows using containers and raised systems placed close together. They sit while tending plants. Tasks are completed in short sessions. The garden remains manageable even during busy or low-energy days.

The difference is not dedication.
The difference is design.

For gardens grown through Grateful Hearts Givings NJ Nonprofit, elevated systems also offer practical advantages. They are easier to monitor, easier for volunteers to assist with, and easier to maintain consistently. When multiple people help, clarity and accessibility matter.

Avoiding the ground does not reduce yield. It often increases it—because the garden receives regular attention instead of sporadic care.

Scripture in Practice

"Make level paths for your feet, so that the lame may not be disabled, but rather healed." — Hebrews 12:13

Wise paths preserve strength and allow continued movement.

Garden Wisdom

The easier a garden is to tend, the more often it will be tended.

Accessibility is productivity in disguise.

Bringing It Together

Avoiding the ground when you can is one of the most effective ways to protect your future as a gardener. Elevation reduces strain, discourages pests, and conserves energy—making consistent care possible across seasons of change.

This approach aligns with the Grateful Hearts Method™ because it honors both the work and the worker. When gardens are designed thoughtfully, they remain life-giving instead of life-draining.

In the next chapter, we will turn our attention to the foundation beneath every successful garden—soil—and why treating it with respect is essential to long-term abundance.

Pause & Reflect

What parts of your garden could be lifted to reduce strain and improve consistency without sacrificing productivity?

Chapter Eleven

Soil Is Life — Treat It That Way

Why what you build beneath the plant determines everything above it

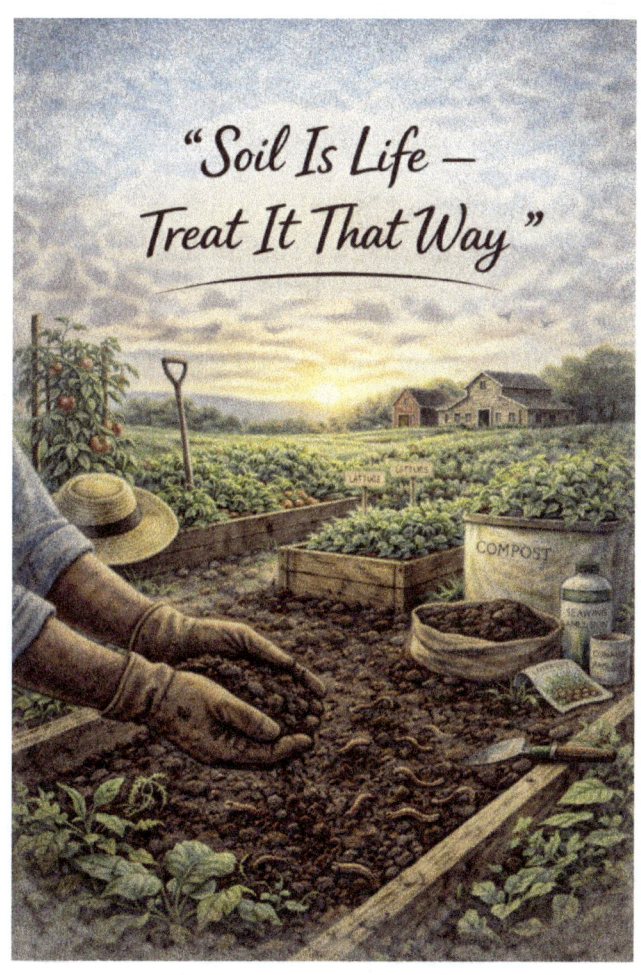

Soil is not dirt.

It is not filler.
It is not a background element.
It is not something to be replaced when it becomes inconvenient.

Soil is alive.

Every successful garden rests on an invisible system of organisms working together—microbes, fungi, bacteria, insects, and organic matter—all interacting in ways that science is still uncovering. When soil is treated as expendable, gardens struggle. When it is treated as living, gardens thrive.

The Grateful Hearts Method™ begins soil care with respect, not products. Healthy soil is not something you purchase once and forget. It is something you build, protect, and nourish over time.

This chapter is about understanding soil as the foundation of abundance—and learning how to care for it without harming what it is designed to support.

Grateful Hearts Principle

Life multiplies where life is honored.

Healthy soil grows strong plants without force.

What You Need to Know

Soil health determines plant health long before leaves appear.

When soil is rich in organic matter and microbial life, plants are better equipped to resist stress, disease, and pests. When soil is depleted, plants become dependent on external inputs to survive.

The goal is not control.
The goal is balance.

Compost is one of the most effective ways to support soil life. Proper composting returns nutrients to the earth while improving structure, moisture retention, and biological activity. Kitchen scraps, garden trimmings, leaves, and plant material all contribute when handled responsibly.

However, composting requires discernment.

Diseased plants should never be added to compost. Doing so risks spreading pathogens throughout future gardens. The Grateful Hearts Method™ teaches gardeners to protect soil by removing infected material completely rather than attempting to recycle it.

Artificial fertilizers may offer quick results, but they often bypass the soil's natural systems. Over time, heavy reliance on artificial inputs weakens microbial life and creates dependency rather than resilience.

This does not mean perfection is required.
It means intentional restraint.

"Do the best you can until you can do better" applies to soil as much as anything else. Use what you have responsibly, improve when possible, and prioritize living systems over shortcuts.

Hard Truth

Soil cannot heal if it is constantly forced.

Quick growth achieved at the expense of soil health leads to long-term loss.

How This Looks in Real Life

A gardener focuses solely on feeding plants. Each season requires more fertilizer, more intervention, and more effort. The soil becomes compacted, lifeless, and unresponsive.

Another gardener feeds the soil instead.

Compost is added gradually. Organic matter is protected. Diseased plants are removed carefully. Artificial inputs are used sparingly, if at all. Over time, the soil improves. Plants grow stronger with less effort.

The difference is patience.

For gardens grown through Grateful Hearts Givings NJ Nonprofit, soil stewardship ensures continuity. Healthy soil reduces costs, increases reliability, and allows gardens to serve year after year without depletion.

Soil that is cared for gives back consistently.

Scripture in Practice

"For the earth yields its crops by itself." — Mark 4:28

Growth happens naturally when conditions are honored.

Garden Wisdom

Feed the soil first.
Plants will follow.

What you build underground determines what you harvest above.

Bringing It Together

Soil is not something to rush or replace. It is something to build gently, protect wisely, and trust over time. When soil is treated as life rather than material, gardens become more resilient and less demanding.

This approach aligns with the Grateful Hearts Method™ because it mirrors stewardship itself—working with creation instead of forcing it.

In the next chapter, we will turn our attention to the human side of gardening: why no one grows sustainably alone, and how building help with integrity strengthens both gardens and people.

Pause & Reflect

What practices in your current gardening approach support soil life—and which might quietly weaken it?

Find this Journal on Amazon
By Joann Comer-Conwell

Chapter Twelve

You Cannot Do This Alone

Why shared work is not weakness, but wisdom

Gardening is often portrayed as a solitary act.

A single person tending rows at sunrise. Quiet work. Independent effort. Self-sufficiency celebrated as virtue. While there is beauty in solitude, there is danger in believing that food production was ever meant to be carried alone.

It was not.

Gardens ask for more than seeds and soil. They ask for time, consistency, observation, strength, and endurance. Even the most capable gardener eventually reaches a point where help is not optional—it is necessary.

The Grateful Hearts Method™ names this truth plainly: sustainable gardens require shared effort. Refusing help does not make a gardener stronger. It makes the garden fragile.

This chapter is about releasing the myth of independence and embracing the wisdom of shared labor.

Grateful Hearts Principle

Strength multiplies when it is shared.

Gardens endure when help is welcomed wisely.

What You Need to Know

No matter how skilled or motivated you are, there will be seasons when you cannot do everything yourself. Weather shifts. Health changes. Life interrupts. Gardens do not pause simply because circumstances become difficult.

Ignoring this reality leads to burnout.

The need for help does not signal failure. It signals growth. As gardens expand, so do their demands. Tasks increase. Timing matters more. The margin for error narrows. At that point, help becomes protection—not dependency.

However, not all help is equal.

The Grateful Hearts Method™ teaches gardeners to build trust slowly. Help should be invited intentionally, not out of desperation. Clear expectations, mutual respect, and shared values create stability. Rushing to accept help without discernment often creates more work than it relieves.

Recognizing real limits is an act of honesty. Overcommitting out of pride places unnecessary strain on both gardener and garden. Accepting help at the right time preserves energy and prevents collapse.

For gardens connected to Grateful Hearts Givings NJ Nonprofit, shared labor also protects mission integrity. Community work must be sustainable. When responsibility rests on one person alone, service becomes fragile. When help is distributed, provision becomes reliable.

Hard Truth

Gardens fail quietly when one person carries everything. Burnout does not announce itself until damage is done.

How This Looks in Real Life

A gardener insists on doing everything alone. At first, the pace is manageable. As the season progresses, tasks accumulate. Missed watering, delayed harvests, and neglected maintenance begin to show. The gardener feels overwhelmed and resentful yet still resists help.

Another gardener plans for assistance.

They invite help early. Tasks are shared in manageable portions. Expectations are communicated clearly. When life interferes—as it inevitably does—the garden continues to function.

The difference is not dedication.
The difference is realism.

For nonprofit gardens, this distinction matters deeply. Volunteers are not optional extras; they are part of the structure that allows the work to continue. When help is treated with respect and clarity, it becomes a source of strength rather than strain.

Scripture in Practice

"Two are better than one, because they have a good reward for their labor." — Ecclesiastes 4:9

Shared work multiplies endurance.

Garden Wisdom

Doing everything yourself limits how far the garden can go.

Help, wisely welcomed, extends both reach and resilience.

Bringing It Together

Gardening was never meant to be a solitary burden. It is a shared act of stewardship, strengthened by cooperation and honesty about human limits.

Accepting help does not diminish your role as a gardener. It protects it. When work is shared, gardens last longer, serve more people, and remain life-giving rather than draining.

In the next chapter, we will explore how generosity must be ordered wisely—why helpers must be honored first, how giving without order breeds bitterness, and how Scripture provides a framework that protects everyone involved.

Pause & Reflect

What tasks in your garden could be shared without losing control—and how might that sharing protect both you and the work?

Do not muzzle an ox while it is treding out the grain: 1 Corinithians 9:9

Chapter Thirteen

"Do Not Muzzle the Ox" – The Order of Giving

Why generosity without order creates resentment

Giving feels simple until it isn't.

In gardens, generosity often begins with excitement and good intentions. There is food. There is abundance. There is a desire to share. But when giving is unstructured, uneven, or rushed, it quietly creates tension that no one expected.

Bitterness rarely begins with selfishness.
It begins with exhaustion.

The Grateful Hearts Method™ teaches that generosity must be ordered to remain healthy. When the order is ignored, helpers feel overlooked, labor is undervalued, and relationships fracture under the weight of silent resentment.

Scripture does not leave this issue vague. It offers a clear principle that protects both giver and receiver: do not muzzle the ox while it treads out the grain.

This chapter is about honoring work honestly—so generosity remains life-giving rather than draining.

Grateful Hearts Principle

Generosity must be ordered to remain joyful.

When labor is honored first, abundance flows without resentment.

What You Need to Know

Food does not appear without effort.

Every harvest represents hours of planning, planting, watering, protecting, observing, and adjusting. When helpers contribute

to that work, their labor becomes part of the harvest itself. Ignoring this truth breaks trust, even when intentions are good.

The Grateful Hearts Method™ establishes a clear order of giving:

First — the helpers.
Those who worked the soil, watered the plants, protected the space, and showed up consistently should receive first. This is not favoritism. It is fairness.

Second — those in need.
Once helpers are honored, provision can be shared outward freely. Giving from a place of balance preserves joy instead of creating quiet sacrifice.

Third — the property owner.
If land was borrowed, gratitude must be expressed tangibly. Sharing harvest acknowledges the trust that made the garden possible.

Fourth — yourself.
The gardener is not last because they are unworthy. They are last because they carry responsibility. Caring for yourself ensures the work continues.

This order is not rigid—it is protective. It prevents helpers from feeling used and gardeners from feeling depleted.

For work done through Grateful Hearts Givings NJ Nonprofit, this order is essential. Volunteers must never feel exploited in the name of service. Honor preserves dignity on all sides.

Hard Truth

Unordered generosity eventually breeds resentment.

People stop helping long before they stop caring.

How This Looks in Real Life

A garden produces generously. Helpers show up faithfully. When harvest comes, everything is given away immediately. Helpers receive little or nothing. Over time, attendance drops. Motivation fades. The garden becomes harder to maintain.

Now consider a different approach.

Helpers harvest first. They take what they need. They feel seen and appreciated. Then the harvest is shared outward. The work continues with joy instead of obligation.

The difference is not the amount of food.
The difference is honor.

For nonprofit gardens, this clarity is vital. When helpers are cared for, the mission strengthens. When they are overlooked, burnout follows.

Scripture's wisdom protects against this outcome.

Scripture in Practice

"You shall not muzzle an ox when it treads out the grain." — Deuteronomy 25:4

Labor deserves acknowledgment before distribution.

Garden Wisdom

If helpers are not honored, help will disappear.

Order preserves generosity.

Bringing It Together

Giving is holy work—but it must be done wisely. When generosity follows order, it remains sustainable. When order is ignored, even good intentions collapse under strain.

The Grateful Hearts Method™ teaches that honoring labor first protects relationships, preserves joy, and ensures abundance continues to flow.

In the next chapter, we will address the practical reality of funding gardens without compromising integrity—why money is part of stewardship and how to raise it without losing your values.

Pause & Reflect

Who contributes to your garden's success—and how are they honored before the harvest is shared?

Chapter Fourteen

Fundraising Without Compromise
Why provision must be planned,
not apologized for

Money is one of the most uncomfortable topics in gardening.

Many people believe that if the work is meaningful enough, it should somehow sustain itself without cost. Others feel that asking for money taints the purity of service. As a result, gardens are often underfunded, under protected, and overextended.

This silence creates unnecessary struggle.

The Grateful Hearts Method™ teaches that money is not the opposite of faith—it is a tool of stewardship. When gardens are expected to serve consistently, they must be supported intentionally. Ignoring financial realities does not make a garden more virtuous. It makes it vulnerable.

This chapter is about removing shame from provision and replacing it with wisdom.

Grateful Hearts Principle

Provision planned with integrity strengthens the work.

Funding does not compromise service—it protects it.

What You Need to Know

Gardens cost money.

Seeds, soil amendments, containers, fencing, tools, pest protection, storage supplies, and maintenance all require resources. Even the most frugal garden depends on some level of financial input.

When funding is not planned, gardeners end up covering costs personally. Over time, this leads to resentment, burnout, or quiet withdrawal from the work. The garden suffers not because the mission failed, but because stewardship was incomplete.

The Grateful Hearts Method™ recommends two intentional fundraising moments per year.

Not constant selling.
Not ongoing pressure.
Two clear, well-planned events.

These events serve multiple purposes:

- They provide necessary funds

- They raise awareness

- They invite community participation

- They create opportunities for volunteers to emerge

When done with clarity and purpose, fundraising becomes a bridge rather than a burden.

For gardens grown through Grateful Hearts Givings NJ Nonprofit, funding also protects accountability. Funds raised publicly can be directed transparently toward supplies, protection, and continuity. This builds trust and reinforces mission integrity.

Hard Truth

Gardens that refuse to plan for money quietly demand it from the gardener.

Unspoken sacrifice eventually becomes unsustainable.

How This Looks in Real Life

A gardener avoids fundraising altogether. Each season, they pay for supplies out of pocket. When costs rise or unexpected needs appear, corners are cut. Protection is delayed. Repairs are postponed. Eventually, exhaustion sets in.

Another gardener plans intentionally.

Two fundraising events are scheduled each year. The purpose is communicated clearly. Funds are used transparently. The garden remains protected, supplied, and stable. The gardener remains energized rather than depleted.

The difference is not generosity.
The difference is foresight.

Fundraising done with integrity does not pressure people—it invites them to participate. It gives supporters a way to invest in something tangible and meaningful.

Scripture in Practice

"Suppose one of you wants to build a tower. Won't you first sit down and estimate the cost?" — Luke 14:28

Wise stewardship plans before building.

Garden Wisdom

Money avoided becomes a silent burden.

Money planned becomes shared responsibility.

Bringing It Together

Fundraising is not a betrayal of faith or mission. It is an acknowledgment of reality. Gardens that are meant to last must be supported honestly and consistently.

The Grateful Hearts Method™ teaches that provision should never be hidden, rushed, or apologized for. When funding is handled with clarity and integrity, it strengthens both the work and the people involved.

In the next chapter, we will face another unavoidable reality of gardening—pests and wildlife—and why protection must be planned rather than reactive.

Pause & Reflect

What costs in your garden are currently unspoken—and how might planning for them protect both you and the work?

Chapter Fifteen

Pests, Wildlife, and Reality
Why protection must be planned, not improvised

Every garden attracts attention.

Some of it is welcome neighbors stopping to admire the growth, children curious about what is planted, helpers eager to learn. Other attention arrives quietly, persistently, and without invitation.

Bugs.
Birds.
Rabbits.
Squirrels.
Deer.

These visitors are not a sign that something has gone wrong. They are evidence that the garden is alive.

The Grateful Hearts Method™ does not treat pests and wildlife as enemies to be eradicated. It treats them as realities to be managed wisely. Ignoring them leads to frustration. Overreacting leads to waste. Wisdom lies in preparation.

This chapter is about learning how to protect what you grow without panic, guilt, or constant crisis.

Grateful Hearts Principle

Protection is part of stewardship.

What is grown with care must also be guarded with wisdom.

What You Need to Know

No garden exists in isolation.

When food is present, life responds. Insects arrive because plants are available. Animals appear because nourishment is nearby. This is not failure—it is ecology.

The mistake many gardeners make is reacting emotionally instead of responding strategically. They try to solve every problem at once, purchase unnecessary products, or abandon the garden entirely after one discouraging loss.

The Grateful Hearts Method™ teaches a different approach: address one problem at a time.

Not every pest requires immediate action. Some damage is cosmetic. Some losses are temporary. Discernment prevents overcorrection.

Protection works best when it is planned before problems escalate. Barriers, covers, deterrents, and physical separation are often more effective than chemical solutions—and far less disruptive to soil life and beneficial insects.

This is where fundraising, discussed in the previous chapter, plays a critical role. Protection costs money. Ignoring this reality leaves gardeners unprepared and reactive.

Hard Truth

Unprotected gardens invite loss.

Repeated loss without a plan leads to discouragement and abandonment.

How This Looks in Real Life

A gardener notices leaves chewed overnight. Panic sets in. Multiple treatments are applied. Plants become stressed. Beneficial insects disappear. The original problem worsens.

Another gardener pauses.

They identify the source of damage. They implement a single, appropriate solution—row cover, physical barrier, or relocation. They observe before acting again. The issue stabilizes.

The difference is not effort.
The difference is restraint.

For gardens grown through Grateful Hearts Givings NJ Nonprofit, protection planning is especially important. When food is grown for others, loss affects more than the gardener. Planning ahead preserves dignity for those depending on the harvest.

Protection is not about control—it is about responsibility.

Scripture in Practice

"The prudent see danger and take refuge." — Proverbs 27:12

Wisdom prepares before loss occurs.

Garden Wisdom

You cannot prevent every loss.

But you can prevent repeated loss through planning.

Bringing It Together

Pests and wildlife are part of the gardening reality. Ignoring them leads to frustration. Fighting them blindly leads to exhaustion. Planning for them leads to balance.

The Grateful Hearts Method™ teaches gardeners to respond with patience, discernment, and preparation. When protection is planned, losses become manageable rather than devastating.

In the final chapter of this book, we will step back and reflect on what the garden gives in return—how it teaches, heals, and reshapes the gardener over time.

Pause & Reflect

What recurring challenges in your garden could be eased by planning rather than reacting?

Closing Chapter

A Garden Grown with Grateful Hearts

Carrying what you've learned forward

By now, you know this book was never just about gardening.

It was about thinking differently before doing.
About protecting what matters before producing more.
About honoring people, land, labor, and provision with integrity.

If you came here looking only for techniques, you likely found something deeper. You found a way of approaching food, work, and stewardship that is slower—but stronger. Simpler—but more durable.

The Grateful Hearts Method™ does not rush growth. It prepares for it.

What Has Been Built

Before a single seed was planted, you learned how to prepare your mind.

You learned why food no longer feels safe—and why that matters.
You learned that gratitude is not sentimental, but foundational.
You learned to begin imperfectly and move forward anyway.
You learned to grow only what you eat, to record what you learn, and to protect memory from loss.

You learned how to see space differently.
How access matters more than ownership.
How integrity is visible before it is trusted.
How clarity in writing protects labor and harvest alike.

You learned to design gardens that honor the gardener.
To lift the work when possible.
To preserve strength for the long run.

You learned that soil is alive.
That help is necessary.
That generosity must be ordered to remain joyful.
That funding, protection, and planning are not compromises—
they are stewardship.

All of this came before abundance.

That was intentional.

Grateful Hearts Principle

What is grown with integrity lasts.

What is rushed without protection fades.

What the Garden Gives Back

Some lessons cannot be learned from pages alone.

As you apply what you've read, the garden will begin to teach you back.

It will teach patience—because growth obeys timing, not urgency.
It will teach humility—because not everything can be controlled.
It will teach attentiveness—because small changes matter.
It will teach healing—because tending life restores something in the soul.

Many gardeners discover that time spent in the garden calms anxiety, steadies emotions, and restores focus. This is not accidental. Creation responds to care, and those who care are often changed in return.

The garden gives back in ways that go beyond harvest.

Scripture in Practice

"Those who sow with tears will reap with songs of joy." — Psalm 126:5

Faithful work, done with patience, brings fruit in its season.

Carrying This Forward

The Grateful Hearts Method™ is not something you finish.

It is something you practice.

You will return to these principles again and again—sometimes to confirm what you already know, sometimes to remember what you forgot, and sometimes to correct what drifted.

That is normal.

Stewardship is not static. It grows as you grow.

This book has given you a foundation. What you build on it will be shaped by your space, your season, your health, and your calling. There is no single right expression—only faithful ones.

A Word About What Comes Next

This is the end of Book One, but it is not the end of the method.

The next stage focuses on what happens after structure is in place—how abundance is carried forward, how harvest is preserved, and how provision continues beyond one season.

You are now prepared for that work.

Not because you know everything.
But because you know what matters first.

Garden Wisdom

Gardens do not grow strong by accident.

They grow strong when hearts are grateful and hands are faithful.

Final Reflection

As you close this book, consider this:

What kind of garden do you want to grow—not just in soil, but in life?

One driven by urgency?
Or one guided by integrity?

One that burns out quickly?
Or one that endures?

The Grateful Hearts Method™ invites you to choose the second path.

Grow slowly.
Grow wisely.
Grow with gratitude.

A Note on Continuity

The Grateful Hearts Method™ is not a single book approach.

This first volume focused on structure before production—because without protection, abundance collapses.

Future volumes will build on this foundation, exploring:

- Carrying harvest forward
- Preservation and storage
- Teaching others
- Building continuity across years

You are prepared for what comes next because you started correctly.

About the Author

JoAnn Comer-Conwell is a faith-rooted gardener, teacher, and founder of Grateful Hearts Givings NJ Nonprofit 501(c) (3). Her work centers on growing and sharing real food in ways that honor God, respect people, and protect the labor behind every harvest.

Through hands-on gardening, community partnerships, and practical teaching, JoAnn helps others learn how to grow clean, chemical-free food even when starting with limited space, resources, or strength. Her approach emphasizes integrity, stewardship, and gratitude as the foundation for lasting abundance.

JoAnn's gardening philosophy is shaped by lived experience—working on borrowed land, organizing shared gardens, feeding those in need, and building systems that protect both people and harvests. She believes food should be grown the way God intended it to be grown thoughtfully, honestly, and with care for both the earth and one another.

She lives and gardens in New Jersey, where her work through Grateful Hearts Givings NJ Nonprofit continues to serve individuals, families, and communities, with a focus on senior citizens and those in need who are seeking healthier food and a more faithful way forward.

About Grateful Hearts Givings NJ Nonprofit

Grateful Hearts Givings NJ Nonprofit exists to restore trust in food, dignity in service, and integrity in stewardship.

Through community gardens, education, and outreach, the nonprofit works to ensure that real food is grown and shared with care, clarity, and respect.

Grateful Hearts Givings NJ Nonprofit prioritizes senior citizens and individuals facing food insecurity, recognizing that access to nourishing food is not a privilege, but a necessity. Its work is rooted in practical action—growing food, sharing harvests, teaching sustainable methods, and building community partnerships that protect both people and the land.

The nonprofit operates with a commitment to ethical growing, fair sharing, and thoughtful stewardship, believing that how food is grown and given matters just as much as the food itself. Every garden, lesson, and act of service is guided by gratitude, integrity, and faith.

This book is one extension of that mission.

Grow slowly.
Grow wisely.
Grow with grateful hearts.

All titles can be found on
amazon.com
under author
JoAnn Comer-Conwell

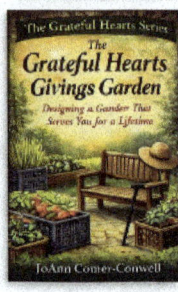 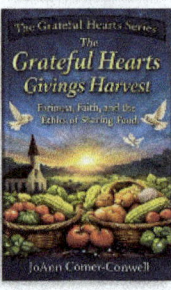 

www.ingramcontent.com/pod-product-compliance
Lightning Source LLC
Chambersburg PA
CBHW050910160426
43194CB00011B/2354